THIS BOOK
BELONGS TO

Vicky Rasinske

COLOR TEST

Basic tips of Drawing!

★ A little bit of art theory is always good to know, Lets start........

★ All you need is a pencil,eraser and a piece off paper!

★ Draw lightly at first because you might need to erase some lines as you work.

★ Add details according to the diagrams but dont worry about being perfect. Artists frequently make mistakes they just find ways to make their mistakes look interesting.

★ Dont worry if your drawing dont turn out the way you want them to , just keep practicing ! Sometimes drawing the same thing just a few times will help.

★ Once you have finished your drawing in pencil you can trace it with a black fineliner pen and color or paint it to your liking.

Turn the page for some cool composition ideas!!!

Please consider writing a review!

THANK YOU